LET ME OUT

Michael Wolliston

INDEX

1, MR THOMAS

"Danburg Police here, how can I help you?"

 "Yes, good evening sir, my name is Helga Schneider and I am a very old woman. My feet are hurting, so I went to the pharmacy, but unfortunately it was already closed!"

"Sorry, Mrs Schneider, but we are the police and are only here for emergencies."

"But this is an emergency... my feet are hurting!" said the old woman. "Can't you open the shop for me again? You are the police! Last week my friend told me how one of you helped her across the street!"

"I'm really sorry, but in this case, we can't help you."

"But what am I supposed to do?" she asked. "I can't walk anymore!"

"Then stay where you are, order a taxi and go home... then put your feet in cold water!"

"Oh, that's a good idea! Many thanks for your help! What is your name young man?"

"My name is Mr Winkler and I wish you a nice evening."

"Oh, thank you, I..."

Officer Winkler hung the phone up. He closed his eyes and knocked his desk three times gently with his head. That was the life of Officer Winkler. Almost every day he got calls from people like the old woman. Whether they were old or young, some of them didn't have *all the cups in the cupboard.* Others were just lonely.

Eyes now open again, he breathed out deeply and looked through the window of his office. In the main office, he could see many other police officers working at their desks.

The commissioner walked into the room. Almost all the men suddenly stood up to greet their boss.

The commissioner smiled. "Sit down gentlemen and please keep working! I've already said that I'm not your president and every time I come to this office; you shouldn't stand up for me!"

The woman was quite beautiful and slim, with typical blonde hair that you could buy from a bottle in a pharmacy. She looked like the mother of a Barbie doll, Officer Winkler often thought. Almost all the men fancied her, whether they were married or not.

"Commissioner Wessler, would you like a cup of tea?" one of the men asked.

"Yes thanks," she replied. "Black with three spoons of sugar, please."

"Good evening Mrs Wessler," said one of the few women in the office.

"Please Sandra... call me Tanja!" said the boss, a bit annoyed. She approached the policewoman and spoke quietly: "Us women must stick together!"

The commissioner suddenly turned around and smiled at Officer Winkler through his office window.

But Officer Winkler didn't smile back. He was probably the only man in the office who didn't like the commissioner at all. But he was a professional and believed that you should always work well together, whether you get along or not.

The phone on his desk rang again.

"Hello, Danburg Police here, how can I help you?"

"Hello, it's about my neighbors from upstairs," a man replied.

"Your neighbors? What about them?" asked Officer Winkler.

"They make a lot of noise every day. I think they wanted to break through my ceiling."

"Wait a minute. You said THEY WANTED... what happened to them?"

"They're dead."

"Dead? Are they really dead?"

"Well... almost dead."

"What do you mean *almost dead*? Please get to the point!" demanded Officer Winkler.

"I'm supposed to get to the point? Then listen to me carefully... if you don't talk to them and the noise doesn't stop, they'll be dead in 90 minutes. Dead...dead… completely dead."

"You want to kill your neighbors in 90 minutes?"

"It would be my pleasure! Or would you rather I do it faster? That wouldn't be a problem for me."

The words KEYWORD RECOGNIZED displayed on Officer Winkler's computer screen. He pressed a red button on his table and spoke: "We'll talk to your neighbors right away! So, what's your address?" He looked for a pen on the table.

"My address? You have my phone number... use it and get here before 90…no…89 minutes have passed."

BOOM!

"Man! What was that?" asked Officer Winkler in shock.

"That was my dear neighbors. As I said, they make a lot of noise and want to break through my ceiling. Now do you see what I mean? You never have any peace here!"

"Okay... I have your address and the police are on their way," said Officer Winkler.

"How long do they need to get here?"

"Not long... about ten minutes. My name is Mr Winkler, what's your name?"

"Please don't ask me. We aren't and won't be friends," the man replied.

"Okay, but you called us. My first name is Martin and I want to help you."

"I prefer to call you Mr Winkler, and your time is running out. Now you have 87 and a half minutes left."

"Yes, but now you have my full name... what's yours?" asked Officer Winkler again.

"You don't need my name. If you have my phone number, then you should know almost everything about me. And now stop asking stupid questions and do your job!"

Sandra and the commissioner hurried in from the main office. They stood next to Officer Winkler. It was clear to him that at least one of them wanted to say something.

Sandra quickly wrote a note on a piece of paper and showed it to him. *WE NEED MORE INFORMATION... WE CAN'T FIND HIS ADDRESS!*

Even though he was sitting in front of his computer, Officer Winkler wrote something back on the same sheet... *WHY NOT?*

Sandra wrote quickly... *HIS PHONE NUMBER HAS CHANGED THREE TIMES!*

"Hello?" asked the man. "Are you still there?"

"Yes... yes, I'm still here," Officer Winkler replied, "but we can't play this game with you anymore!"

"But this isn't a game..." the man responded calmly.

"Okay, listen to me... I made a mistake, and we can't find where you are. What is your address? Without it, we can't stop the noise... please!"

"The woman argues with her husband almost every day," was the man's only answer.

"Every couple sometimes argue, but that's no reason to kill them!" said Officer Winkler aloud. The official suddenly jumped up and pointed at the loudspeaker on his desk. "Tell me your name! If you don't tell me it, I'll call you Mr THOMAS!"

"But that's not my name."

"Mr THOMAS, what exactly do you want from us?" the official asked.

The man breathed in deeply and then slowly out. "I usually work in my living room and in the afternoon, the neighbors' children come home..."

"And?"

"... and Mr Winkler, they play a lot of video games and their stupid TV is always very, very loud. Why buy such a huge TV? It's 92 inches. The small improvement in the picture quality isn't worth all that extra money. All you get is a lot more noise!"

"All TVs make noise!" shouted Officer Winkler.

"True, but there are six floors in this building... and I'm very sure that most of the noise comes from them!"

"Mr THOMAS, are the parents there as well?" asked Officer Winkler. He sat back on his chair.

"Excuse me?"

"I mean, when the kids come home, are the parents there as well?"

"The father is unemployed and almost always with them," the man replied.

"Really? How do you know that the father is unemployed?"

"Officer Winkler, my neighbors talk very, very loud and I'm not deaf. When we both turn off our TVs, I can hear almost everything they say!"

"Mr THOMAS, I understand you now. The man is unemployed, but his wife works and when she comes home, there are usually arguments?"

"Correct Mr Winkler! Arguments like, *why hasn't the house been tidied? Or I've been working hard, what exactly have you done today?* and so on."

"And that's why the kids turn the TV volume up?" the official asked.

"Correct again! They don't want to hear their parents arguing."

"Mr THOMAS, please can you..."

"My name is MEIER!... MR MEIER! understand?" the caller shouted. "M - E - I - E - R! If you call me *MR THOMAS* again, I swear that I'll shoot the woman right now!"

"Okay... Okay... stay calm Mr Tho... er... Mr Meier, stay calm!" said Officer Winkler.

THUD!

"You have 84 minutes left. Are the police coming soon, or not? You haven't said a word about them for a while! Haven't they found my address yet?"

"Yes... I mean no... our tech department can't find it."

"Well that means this phone is working correctly... the number changes four or five times every minute, doesn't it? Finally, I bought something useful on the Dark Web!"

The officers looked at each other.

"And what is the commissioner doing right now?" asked Mr Meier, interrupting their silence. "Is she with you or is she drinking her cup of English tea, as always?"

"I was drinking tea when you called us," said the commissioner over the loudspeaker. "Now listen to me.

You've had your fun, now answer us and let's finish this stupid game!"

"Oh Mr Winkler, how sweet it is when the boss speaks... or is it just her teeth that are sweet? Does she still like three spoons of sugar in her tea?"

"Hey! You're talking as if I'm not here!" the boss protested.

Sandra went quickly and sat at the second computer, next to Officer Winkler.

"And dear people..." Mr Meier began, "…before you continue to search for me... a little clue for you all... I'm not an ex-policeman. I'm just trying to help you."

"But..."

"There is no *but*, ladies and gentlemen. I've only seen your wonderful police station on a TV report, just like another 16,000 viewers."

Sandra got up again, quite disappointed. She was sure that he was speaking the truth. Three months ago, their station was shown in a television documentary.

"Who are you then?" asked Officer Winkler.

"The woman argues with her husband almost every day," he replied briefly.

"We already know that! Tell us something new, or at least tell us your address!" demanded Officer Winkler.

"*Something new*? Okay I can do that... the husband argues almost every day... with his wife!" He paused, while no one laughed and then continued, but this time very seriously: "It makes me very sad to hear the two of them arguing every day.

My parents are both dead. They never argued but loved each other until their death."

Officer Winkler took a deep breath and breathed out loudly. The conversation was going nowhere. For a moment, he thought about the situation and then sat up. "Mr Meier... how loud is it where you are, right now?" he asked suddenly.

"Now? It's not that bad tonight because their TV isn't that loud. Why are you asking me?"

"Isn't *that loud,* you say? But it's already eight o'clock! Isn't the wife at home?"

"Hmmmm... no. No, she's not at home."

"Really?" said Officer Winkler surprised. "But that doesn't make sense. If it's not that loud this evening, why are you calling us?"

"That's a good question. Today's my birthday and so I didn't want to have any noise this evening."

"I still don't understand you."

"I just wanted to have a bit of peace, that means no noise and no daily arguments, like during the last two months since they moved here."

"But Mr Meier, when the wife comes back, it will be loud again!" said Officer Winkler.

"*Be loud again*? No, not this evening... this evening it will be quite quiet. Do you want to talk to her?"

"Oh no, please don't go upstairs to your neighbors!" shouted Officer Winkler alarmed.

"*Upstairs*? No, no, no. She's right here, lying on my bed… one moment please."

Officer Winkler, the commissioner and Sandra looked at each other, again speechless.

2. "TWO?"

With his mobile phone still in his hand, Mr Meier slowly walked to his bed and sat on it. Next to him lay a very beautiful and slim woman… with her hands and feet tied behind her back.

"Mr Winkler, here's my neighbor," said Mr Meier. He yawned and then moved his face next to the face of the motionless woman. "Dear Neighbor, because it's my birthday today, you may talk to the police briefly. So, Mrs Neighbor, do you argue with your husband, almost every day?"

"Yes, I argue with my husband almost every day!" she replied quickly with a mixture of fear and tears.

"And tomorrow morning, if you're still alive, what would you want to do?"

"I would spend the whole day with my husband!" she replied loudly. "I would kiss him and would never again..."

Mr Meier gently pressed his finger against her lips. "That's enough."

The commissioner wrote something on a new page and quickly showed it to Officer Winkler. *SAY TWICE, "HELLO ARE YOU STILL THERE?" AND THEN HANG UP.*

Officer Winkler looked at his boss, quite confused by her order. But orders are orders...

"Hello, are you still there?" asked Officer Winkler.

"Yes, I'm still here..."

"Hello... Mr Meier, are you still there?" asked Officer Winkler again.

"Hello?" replied Mr Meier, "What's wrong with you?"

But Officer Winkler had already ended the telephone conversation, as the commissioner had ordered him to.

"What do we do now?" he asked the commissioner.

"He's playing a crazy game with us, but he didn't expect us to hang up! I have an idea. Call the phone company quickly... Sandra, how long did the conversation with Mr Meier last?"

"Exactly 9 minutes and 42 seconds..." Sandra replied.

The phone company's assistant immediately replied: "Good evening, Danburg Telecom here, the choice of the Federal Repub..."

"Enough!" interrupted the commissioner. "Please send us all the information about a call, which lasted exactly 9 minutes and 42 seconds, but that happened only within the last 11 minutes!"

"One moment..." said the assistant at the other end. "Oh dear... there were two."

"*Two*?" asked the commissioner. "There were two calls that lasted exactly that amount of time? Damn!" she shouted and hit the table hard. Officer Winkler and Sandra both jumped back with shock. The boss then continued: "... okay, okay... stay calm. Do you have the information for both of them?"

"Yes, we have. I'm sending them over to your computer now."

"Thank you for your help," said the commissioner.

"My pleasure... and apologies for my long greeting. I'm new here and I would have..."

Sandra pressed a button on the desk that ended the conversation for the commissioner. Very rude, but necessary in this case.

"Okay we now have the two numbers," she said, "The first call came from *a Mr Hagen*. He lives alone... works at Siemens and has a daughter called Matilda. The phone call came from Tempelhofer Garten. His house, that..."

"Stop!" the commissioner interrupted. "We're looking for someone who lives in a tower block building... please check the second number."

"Sure... the second number on the list comes from a *Mr Blond*. He has no brothers or sisters, but has three cats... The address is Danburg, 189 Heilige Strasse and the phone number is: *zero, one, two... Um... three... four*? Hey, what the heck is this?"

"Man, oh man," said Officer Winkler. "*Five, six and seven*. Surely this number belongs to our man, but it's no good to us!"

"We are on the wrong track," said the commissioner disappointedly. She sat slowly next to Officer Winkler. After a few seconds, she suddenly turned to him: "You've done well up to now. But he's told us so much, that I can't believe he hasn't given us any clues. Please repeat everything we know about him so far."

"His name is Mr Meier. The tower block in which he lives has six floors. His neighbors above him have children. The father is unemployed. They often argue and make a lot of noise..." said the official. "They have more than one child. Their children are probably teenagers because they play their video games every day... they moved in two months ago... Er... we don't know anything else."

"Yes, we do!" the commissioner suddenly shouted excitedly. She jumped up again. "Yes, he also talked about the noise of the video games coming from their huge TV! That's the clue! How often would anyone in this town buy such a large TV? Hardly ever?"

"You're right," replied Officer Winkler. "It's 92 inches wide. I would say that only a few of them have ever been bought."

"Exactly! Start looking for them! "ordered the commissioner. "I want at least five officers working on it... immediately!"

"But commissioner, it could have been bought on the internet!" said Sandra.

"I don't think so," said Officer Winkler. "Think about it... anyone spending that much money on an electronic device, would certainly want to see it working in a shop. Usually such a large TV can only be bought in a big department store, such as Media Markt or Saturn."

"You're wasting our time!" said the commissioner. "Start searching now!" she ordered again, but this time louder. Immediately, six officers started making phone calls. After five minutes they had found two buyers, but one of them had brought the device back because it was too heavy to hang on their wall.

The other buyer was the Danburg Police... the crime scene department... how embarrassing!

"Commissioner!" shouted Sandra excitedly. "We've just found a third buyer! Almost two months ago, a buyer named Petra Jacobvic bought such a large TV!"

"And what makes her so special?"

"She bought two video games at the same time, for the two boys who were with her," the policewoman replied. "The salesman remembers her very well, because she looked very beautiful and also because she paid for everything in cash!"

"But does she have a husband? And was he also there?"

"Yes, and he argued with her the whole time about how much money she wanted to spend..."

"That must be them! Okay, the search is over. Finally, we can look for more information about this man. We..."

"Already on it..." interrupted Sandra, looking at the computer screen, "... and yes... there he is... we've found him! Petra Jacobvic's husband is *Filip Jacobvic*. He is unemployed and has a mobile phone which is paid for by his wife," she said. "We can also see their TV and other mobile phone contracts... their address is Hermannstraße 92, 01067 Danburg."

"That fits..." said Officer Winkler, "and there are calls between the two of them almost daily. Now we definitely have the husband's phone number, but he still has to confirm everything."

Sandra called the number. "It's ringing..." she said.

"Hello?" answered a man with a very deep voice.

"Hello, here is the Danburg Police…"

"The Danburg Police?... Hahaha, very funny!" He laughed and hung up.

Sandra called the phone number again.

"Hello?" replied the man again.

"Please don't hang up!" asked Sandra. "We really are the police, and we need to talk to you!"

"Young woman, don't joke with me, I'm..."

"It's about your wife," she interrupted.

"My wife? What do you mean by that? Is she alright? Has she done something wrong?"

"We believe she's ok and hasn't done anything wrong, but we must quickly confirm that you are the man we're looking for."

"What?"

"Firstly... what is your surname?"

"Jacobvic... J A C O B V I C ... please don't joke with me. Are you really the police?"

"Yes, we are, and we don't have much time. Please answer me, only with *yes* or *no*."

"Okay, I will... but is my wife in danger?"

"Mr Jacobvic, you must answer our questions. It is very important that you help us. Is your wife's name Petra Jacobvic?"

"Oh God, yes, that's her name!"

"Have you seen her in the last half an hour?"

"No, she's not with me."

"And is that normal for her? At this time?" asked Sandra.

"Err, actually no. It's eight o'clock. Normally she would call me if she had to work overtime."

"Okay... and do you have children?"

"Yes, two boys who are now playing with their stupid video games. The boys are fine, but tell me now... what's the matter with my wife?"

"We'll explain everything to you soon, but we have another question... and excuse me for having to ask, but are you unemployed?"

"How do you know that I...? Ok. Yes... yes, I'm unemployed! Are you happy now?"

"Just a moment please" said Sandra. She pressed a button, so that the man couldn't hear her voice.

"He's definitely the husband of the kidnapped woman," she said to Officer Winkler and the commissioner.

"I have to make a call," said the commissioner quietly, leaving the office.

"Hello?" said the man.

Sandra didn't want to scare the man. She would have to lie to him. She released the button and said: "Okay, we think your wife is okay, but we need to check your apartment. What is your address?"

"You're lying!" he shouted back. "Tell me the truth! I have fully cooperated with you. Tell me what's the matter with her!"

"Mr Jacobvic, we need your address, it is very important! We can explain everything to you when you and your children have left the apartment."

"You're not getting my address until you tell me about my wife!"

"Listen to me carefully…" said Sandra, "if we are late because of you, and something bad happens to your wife, how would you explain that to your children?"

"Er, my address is Hermannstraße 92, 01067 Danburg."

"And what is your apartment number and which floor do you live on?"

"Apartment 409, on the fourth floor."

Sandra and Officer Winkler looked up as the commissioner came back into the office. She had heard everything on her headset and gave them the thumbs up.

"Thank you, we've now confirmed everything," said Sandra on the phone. "Now go outside with your children straight away and close the door. We'll be there soon."

"Okay... Guys come here! We have to leave right away!"

"Mr Jacobvic, it's important that you don't end this call when you're outside. Go now!"

The man turned to his children. The boys were still playing their video games. "Markus, Thomas! ... I'm serious! Turn the TV off and let's go!" he said louder.

"Don't turn off the TV!" shouted Sandra and Officer Winkler at the same time. They looked at each other briefly and then looked back at the speaker on the table.

"Excuse me? I shouldn't turn it off?" asked the man confused. "But you just said we have to leave!"

"I know it's a weird request," said the policewoman, "but trust me and leave the TV on."

"Why can't he turn it off?" the commissioner asked Officer Winkler quietly.

"Because Mr Meier would notice that there's suddenly no more noise upstairs!" he answered. "He probably lives directly under the family on the third floor, in apartment 309. The police are nearly there."

"Okay, we're going, and I'll leave the TV..." said Mr Jacobvic, still on his phone, "... I'll just turn down the volume a bit."

"No! Don't touch it!" shouted Sandra.

"Mr Meier will probably call us back very soon," said the commissioner. "I don't think he'll be happy until someone dies!"

"BOYS!" screamed the father suddenly at his shocked children. "Are you deaf? We have to get out of here right away!"

Finally, the three started to leave the living room.

"We only have 55 minutes," she said. "We need to warn the other people in the tower block."

"But if we do that, Mr Meier will know that something is happening," warned Officer Winkler.

And just at that moment, his phone rang. Sandra answered. "It's Mr Meier again," she said quietly.

"Hello Mr Meier! Thank God we are reconnected!" said Officer Winkler friendlily, despite hating the man.

"Shut up, Mr Winkler. What have you just done?"

"We are still searching for your address," the official lied again.

Sandra was now in her own office, still on the line with Mr Jacobvic. Her office was next to Officer Winkler's. She was on her own, so that Mr Jacobvic couldn't hear anything about his kidnapped wife. "Are you all outside now?" she asked him.

"Yes, we are."

BEEP!

"Please move further away. Maybe there's a café nearby?"

"Excuse me? You want me to go and drink a latte or cappuccino while my wife is in danger?" he asked in shock.

"Um..." said Sandra, unsure of what to say.

"I'm waiting opposite the tower block and I'm not going any further!" said the man.

BEEP BEEP!

Sandra now noticed the "BEEP" tone. Surely it came from a phone near her. *"Man, oh man... who's calling me now?" she thought. "Two calls at the same time? How is that even possible?"* She looked at her phone's display, but everything looked fine.

"Hello Mrs Officer..." Mr Jacobvic said suddenly.

"Yes?"

BEEP! BEEP!

"My phone isn't charged... the battery is very weak. I can..."

"Write down my number quickly!" interrupted Sandra, "0175..."

BEEP! BEEP!

"I said that my battery is weak!" the man shouted, now very angry. "Giving me your number doesn't help me! And you call yourself a policewoman? Because of you, I still don't know what's happened to my wi ..."

BEEP! BEEP! BEEP! BEEP! BEEP!

The connection terminated.

Sandra didn't want to get herself into trouble for what had just happened. She considered what to do. Finally, she knew what to tell the commissioner. She would say that Mr Jacobvic had suddenly ended the call. That wouldn't be a complete lie... would it?

Back in the office next door, the situation wasn't much better...

"Mr Winkler, I am not stupid," warned Mr Meier. "I know you've planned something. Do you really want to shoot me on my birthday?"

"Of course not," Officer Winkler lied again. "We don't want anyone to die, but..."

"But in 49 minutes this woman... my dear, beautiful neighbor, will be dead," Mr Meier interrupted.

"Don't do it," begged Officer Winkler.

"What? *Don't do it,* did you say?" Mr Meier began to laugh hysterically. "Ha ha ha ha! You are very funny Mr Winkler... hah ha hah! I haven't laughed this much in years... *Don't do it* ... ha ha ha!"

Mr Meier continued to laugh. He laughed so much that for a moment he could hardly breathe. He coughed loudly and then slowly breathed in and out five or six times to calm himself down.

At last he felt better and didn't laugh as hysterically as before. "Okay, Mr Winkler... ha ha ha ha! ... Ok... as you wish... I won't do it."

"Promise?" asked Officer Winkler, surprised.

"Ha ha ha, erm... yes, promise... I won't kill the woman in 46 minutes. You have my word... *Don't do it*... ha ha ha!"

He hung up.

"Hello?" said Officer Winkler, but he didn't get an answer. *"That was very sudden!"* thought the officer. *"Is it really over now? Will Mr Meier release the poor woman? ... and just like that?"*

3. THE S.E.K.

Officer Winkler stood up. He had to go and see the commissioner. She was in her office on a telephone call, not with the police, but with the Leader of the Special Operations Commandos (SEK). He was waiting outside near Hermannstraße with his armed men.

"We can't have a shootout in a tower block full of residents!" shouted the commissioner.

"Of course I agree," said the SEK leader, "but if we don't go in and the woman dies, then the world media will say that we, the German police, have no desire to protect foreigners!"

"That may be, but imagine what would happen if not all the Germans had left the tower block, and some of them died in a shootout? Then everyone would say: *Oh, so 20 policemen jump up and run off to protect a foreigner, while a few innocent Germans die!* What then?"

"Hey, the woman is just as innocent!" the SEK leader shouted. "No one is directly threatening the residents. If the alarms go off, they can leave the building, but the woman can't. We have to go in quickly!"

The commissioner paused and exhaled loudly. "You know what? In this case, no one can win, but it's better that we do something, instead of nothing and just crossing our fingers.

Okay, you can enter, but first give the residents ten minutes to leave the building."

"Ten minutes? Yeah okay," replied the SEK leader. "The fewer residents remaining in the building, the better. And whoever is stupid enough to ignore ten minutes of alarms, can't complain to the police. I will..."

"Wait a moment," the commissioner interrupted. "Officer Winkler has just walked in with more news."

Officer Winkler approached the table with the phone on it and spoke: "Mr Meier has suddenly changed his mind. He just promised me not to shoot the woman."

"Really??" asked the commissioner and the SEK leader at the same time.

"Whether he's serious or not, we have to save the woman quickly," said the SEK leader.

"Okay," said the commissioner, "as planned... your men will activate the fire alarm in the building and the technician will make some smoke with his smoke machine. With a little luck, all residents will have left the building after that."

"Quick, let's get going!"

The plan began at once. On all the floors (except the third), the police smashed the small glass boxes and activated the fire alarms. These officers in the building weren't wearing uniform but were dressed just like the residents of the tower block.

"FIRE, FIRE!" they shouted. "We have to get out of here!"

The residents started to come out of their apartments into the corridors.

"What's going on here?" a man asked.

"There's a fire upstairs!" lied a policewoman. "Get out of the building. Quick!"

"*Get out of the building?* Who are you? I've never seen you here before!" he replied.

"I live upstairs," she lied again. "I'm going to knock on a few more doors and then I'm getting out too!"

"Hey, I can smell smoke!" another man screamed. "I'm getting out of here, straight away! ... Eva... Come quickly! We have to get out of here!"

On the third floor no fire alarm had been activated because it was too dangerous, but almost everybody could hear the other alarms as well as lots of shouting. Many looked out of their windows. Below they could see three fire engines... and a police car.

Mr Meier also looked out of his window. He saw the fire engines, the many residents and the single police car. He continued to study the situation and then suddenly smiled. Finally, he stepped back from the window and turned to the woman. "Dear neighbor, I think the police are trying to save you. The fun has finally begun! Did I say: *The fun has finally begun*? Oh, you know what I mean!"

He laughed quietly to himself and looked out the window again, but this time only through the curtains.

He coughed. "The smoke is bothering me. I need a bit of fresh air. But first I have a question for you... just how comfortable do you find my bed?"

Petra Jacobvic didn't answer him. She knew what would happen if she said something that he didn't like.

"It's okay. You may answer my question," he assured her. As he spoke, he took out a small knife from his pocket and began removing some dirt from under a fingernail with it.

"I... I don't know what to say!" Petra replied with fear.

Mr Meier laughed quietly as he removed the dirt from under another fingernail. "I'm sure the best tactic is to always tell the truth. So, I'll ask you again... just how comfortable do you find my bed?" He turned directly to the woman and waited for her answer.

"It... It... it's better than mine!" she said quickly, and then tightly closed her eyes.

"Better than yours? Is that all? Dear neighbor, my bed has the best memory foam in the world! Do you really think there's a better bed in this building?"

"Um... no."

"We'll see," he said quietly. "We'll see." Mr Meier put the knife back into his pocket and clapped his hands. "Okay, let's go and find another apartment!"

"What?"

"I said we were going to another apartment."

"Another apartment? But why?"

"I ask the questions, okay? Only me. But if you really have to know... firstly, maybe it is not clever to stay in the apartment directly below yours... and secondly, because I really want to prove to you that I have the best bed!"

Petra opened her mouth to ask something else, but then she remembered what he had just said. She closed her mouth and said nothing.

"Good!" said Mr Meier, impressed. "You finally followed my wish! Okay, listen to me carefully... I am going put you in this large furniture box and put some clothes and newspapers on top of you. Then I'll push it until we can find an open apartment... very simple and quite exciting! Isn't it?"

"But..."

"Oh, you want to know what would happen if you move inside the box, so that someone notices? Easy... you would die. Just like if you screamed. The fire alarms are still very loud, so it would be hard to hear a small gunshot. Do you understand me?"

"I won't move or scream, I promise you!" said Petra quickly. "But there's a fire here and if you stayed in the building and pushed a big box like that, don't you think that would look suspicious? The fire brigade would contact the police straight away!"

Mr Meier smiled at the woman. "Dear neighbor, I didn't know that you were so worried about my well-being! Okay, shut up now! You bore me very much, despite your beauty."

.

4. PHOTOS

The smoke was now everywhere in the tower block. Many residents on the third floor were rushing through the corridors. They all could now see and smell the smoke.

"Fire! Let's get out of here!" many of them screamed.

"The stupid fire alarms here didn't work!" shouted a running man. "What do we pay our taxes for? The government should protect us!"

"Don't forget what happened two years ago, in the building across the street!" shouted another man, wearing only his underpants. "I'm not waiting here until I see the fire!" Despite his lack of clothes, he, like the other residents, quickly left the building.

More and more residents on the third floor were running out quickly. But one young woman ran with difficulty through the crowd in the opposite direction.

"Hey!" shouted a man standing in her way. "Where are you going? The exit isn't that way!"

"Out of my way, please!" she shouted as she ran around him.

Finally, she got to her apartment. She opened the door with her key and quickly went inside. From her bedroom she collected her mobile phone charger and iPad.

Back at the apartment door, she searched for her keys, but couldn't find them in her pockets. Someone nearby screamed.

The woman turned around scared and immediately began running back towards the main exit.

Like many other residents, she had closed her door, but hadn't locked it.

———

Just a few minutes had passed since the fire alarms were activated. Opposite the tower block stood many of the residents, including Mr Jacobvic and his children.

"Dad, what's going on here?" asked one of the sons. The father looked at him in amazement.

"There are five fire trucks here Markus! Why do you think they are…?" He suddenly stopped himself and took a slow, deep breath. Despite the stupid question, it would be better if he stayed calm. "Please give me your phone," he finally asked him. "My battery is flat."

"My phone? I can't. I left it next to the TV."

"*Next to the TV*? Why did you do that?"

"I thought we would be going back soon. You didn't tell us that we would have to stay outside!"

The Father stretched out his big hands. "Really Markus? Didn't you think for a moment: *Oh, maybe it would be useful if I took my phone with me*? Man! I know your life consists of Facebook, Instagram, and YouTube, but sometimes people use their phones to make phone calls!"

Markus hung his head, as a man walked over to them.

"Sorry to bother you guys, but do you live in this tower block?" he asked them.

"Yes, who are you?" answered Mr Jacobvic.

"Simon Kreuz is my name, but please call me Simon. I live here too. I have to show you something. About half an hour ago, my girlfriend and I saw a handbag on the main staircase, in which we found these photos. The big man in the photos looks similar to yourself. Please take a look."

He gave Mr Jacobvic a few of the photos. "Right now, my girlfriend has the handbag" he said. "But she'll be back soon."

Mr Jacobvic looked at a photo. His eyes widened. "This is a photo of me and my wife! We took this photo in America last year! Petra... Petra... my god... Is she still somewhere in the building?"

"What do you mean?" asked Simon. "Isn't she out here?"

"I'm not sure now. And she hasn't called me yet." Suddenly, Mr Jacobvic was very worried about his wife. He quickly turned to the children. "Guys... come here! Take this money and go to Café Martha. Stay there until I pick you up... understood? Ok, go quickly!"

"What do you want to do?" asked Simon. "Shouldn't you tell the police?"

But Mr Jacobvic suddenly began to run back to the building, "I have to find her!" he shouted to Simon.

"But you can't go back in there!" Simon shouted back. "You can't... Oh! What the heck. Wait for me ... I'll come with you!" He started to run after his new friend.

"Hey stop! Where are you going?" asked a firefighter. He took a step-in front of them, but Mr Jacobvic was even bigger than in the photos and with just one hand he pushed the firefighter aside and ran on.

The firefighter fell to the ground. "Come back!" he shouted, but both men ignored him and kept on running.

The two men entered the building. "Man!" said Simon, shaking his head, "I can't believe what I just did! That was crazy! Hey, I haven't seen this corridor before. Where are we?"

"This isn't the main entrance, it's the emergency exit," replied Mr Jacobvic.

"Oh! Well then, we don't have much time! Which floor should we search for her first?"

"First in my apartment on the fourth floor and then where you found her bag," Mr Jacobvic replied.

They ran up the stairs. "The smoke here isn't that thick," commented Mr Jacobvic, as the two men arrived_on the fourth floor.

"We have to be quick," said Simon. My girlfriend is expecting a call from me soon."

"Apartment 409. The door isn't locked!" were Mr Jacobvic's only words.

The two hurried into apartment 409. "Please search in the kitchen and in the bathroom," asked Mr Jacobvic. "Petra, Petra!" he shouted, "Petra, are you there?" He continued to search for his wife but didn't find her in either of the bedrooms.

He then went into the living room, where the TV was still on. Annoyed, he turned it off and picked up his son's mobile phone, which was next to it. He dialled his wife's number. For a moment the phone was silent and then: *"Hi I'm Petra*

Jacobvic. Thank you for calling, but unfortunately, I am not available at the moment. Please leave a...”

He hung up, totally frustrated.

“She's not here,” said Simon, now also in the living room. “She's got to be outside somewhere. We really should get out now!”

“I can't go until I'm sure that she's not here!” shouted Mr Jacobvic. “Where exactly did you find the bag?”

“On the second floor,” Simon replied.

“Please show me where exactly, and then get out straight after that. On this side of the building there’s a lift. Let's take it down to that floor.”

“No,” replied Simon “The lift would be very dangerous to take, when there’s a fire. We have to take the stairs! The main exit is also nearby.”

“Yeah okay... you're right!”

The two ran down the stairs and were almost on the third floor.

Suddenly, Mr Jacobvic stood still.

“What's wrong?” asked Simon.

Mr Jacobvic didn’t reply. Just below them on the third floor, in front of a door, there were a lot of photos on the floor. Slowly he approached, went down onto one knee and picked them all up.

“Petra... Aunt Susanna... my god... Thomas, Markus and myself. These photos belong to my wife! She took them all with her mobile phone and printed them out!” He turned to

Simon. "I don't understand... why are our family photos lying on this floor?"

"I don't know," Simon replied. "I'm sorry, but I have to go now. You better leave as well..."

SMASH!

The two men looked up.

"There's someone else still in the building!" said Mr Jacobvic.

The two ran immediately into apartment 309. They looked everywhere, but they couldn't find anyone.

"Nobody's here," said Simon. "I have to go now."

"But..."

FUD! FUD!

This time someone nearby had clearly struck a wall twice.

"Next door!" they both shouted at the same time and immediately ran there. The apartment door next door was also unlocked. Mr Jacobvic ran inside. There were three more doors. He opened the first.

It was a bedroom. The room was very modern, with expensive pictures on the wall, but the large, elegant bed was messy. Strangely, the pillows were missing.

Mr Jacobvic walked to the other side of the bed and there he saw a broken alarm clock on the floor. Next to it, tied by her hands, feet and now also around the mouth, laid his wife.

Tears rolled slowly out of her eyes.

"PETRA!" screamed Mr Jacobvic in shock.

"One more step and you're dead!" interrupted Simon.

Mr Jacobvic froze. In the large mirror he could see that *helpful Simon* now had a gun against his back.

"What kind of stupid man are you?" asked Mr Meier. "Get on the bed... nice and slow!"

"But Simon, I thought you were helping me!" said Mr Jacobvic, quite confused.

"Lie down on your fat belly and shut up!" ordered Mr Meier.

"But what about the fire?... we are..."

"There is no fire in this building, you idiot!" shouted Mr Meier. "The only danger here is me. Understood?" He pointed his gun in the direction of the bed. "Get on the bed" he repeated quietly.

Mr Jacobvic walked over to the bed and slowly laid down on it. "Please let my wife go," he begged.

Mr Meier ignored his request and continued: "Well, dear people, this apartment is colder than mine and we don't want to catch a cold, do we? Maybe I should close the door? Is anyone against that?"

The couple remained quiet.

"Good... very good!" said Mr Meier. He laughed quietly to himself and carefully closed the door.

5. GO!

Outside, in front of the tower block, stood the SEK leader. He was waiting for a special police car. In it were the commissioner and Sandra, on their way to the location.

"Drive faster!" came the order from the back seat.

"I'm driving as fast as I can... commissioner," said Sandra.

"I found the short skirt. But did you bring the shoes and lipstick?" the commissioner asked. She searched the handbag she had with her.

"Yes ma'am, they're in the yellow bag."

"Oh good," said the commissioner relieved. "I'm almost ready, but man oh man! It's so hard to change clothes in a car! How do the young women do it when they're on their way to a club every weekend?"

"No idea," the driver replied. "I don't go to clubs because I'm not a young woman anymore."

The commissioner looked at Sandra but said nothing.

———

The tower blocks residents were now behind a police barrier. Only the police and firefighters were allowed past.

"Something isn't right here," one resident said to her brother.

"Why do you say that?" he asked.

"Look… the firefighters are only spaying the water on the side of the building, but the smoke is everywhere. And look around you… there's almost as many police here as firefighters."

"Oh yeah, you're right!" he said. "That's strange!" He turned around again. "Hey, listen... isn't that another police car coming?"

"So it seems. Something else is going on here."

The police car with Sandra and the commissioner arrived. The back-seat door opened at once, but the commissioner got out carefully, because she had changed into a very short skirt. The SEK leader walked straight past Sandra and went immediately to his boss.

"Commissioner Wessler, what you're now planning to do, is crazy! Why should you go in there alone?"

"Because I've spoken with this guy on the phone and I know these types of men quite well," she replied.

"That isn't a good enough reason for you to enter the building alone... you're not Jane Bond!"

"*Jane Bond*? That's very funny sir, but at the moment there are still residents in the building, and it would be very dangerous for them and the woman, if armed police went in there."

"But..."

"There is no *but*... some of them could be deaf, for example. Until just now, I hadn't thought about that. I'll go in there and if I don't come out with the woman in 15 minutes, send your armed men in."

He stepped closer to the commissioner.

"Tanja... you're crazy. You're almost as crazy as your clothes!" he said quietly. "Why on earth are you dressed like that?"

"Oh Karl, don't you like my outfit?" she asked just as quiet. "I just wanted to look like one of the residents."

"Just go, you crazy woman! You have fifteen minutes to save her and after that my men go in with weapons!"

From behind the police barrier, the brother and sister from earlier watched, as a beautiful middle-aged woman ran with difficulty towards the tower block dressed in crazy nightclub clothing.

"What's the hell is going on?" they asked a nearby policewoman.

"She is our... Um ...she's working with the police."

"But she's..."

"Please don't ask me anymore questions, we have our orders!" she said. She turned around and walked away from the two.

6. GOODNIGHT

The official deadline that Mr Meier had given the police, had now expired. He was talking on the phone again to Officer Winkler.

"Mr Winkler..."

"Yes, Mr Meier?"

"46 minutes have passed, and the woman is still alive."

"Oh, thank God!"

"Why do you sound so surprised? I gave you my word not to kill her within the 46 minutes."

"Yes... and now you're going to let her go?"

"Of course not."

"What? Why not?"

"Mr Winkler, I never said that I wouldn't shoot her *after* the 46 *minutes* had passed. "

"Oh man... Please!... don't do it!"

"*Don't do it*? Ha ha ha! You know what? I'm not sure who's the dumbest... you or Mr Jakabitz?"

"What? You know him?"

"Yes, of course. Mr Jakabitz is here now. He was lonely, so I went outside to get him."

"You went outside? That's not possible!"

"Yes, it was. Because of your smoke machines, I needed a bit of fresh air. While I was outside, I gave someone my phone and he took a photo of me and a policewoman. Then I went to meet Mr Jakabitz and his lovely children."

"Oh man, that's totally crazy! Why are you doing this?"

"I'm doing it because it's fun. Do you know what fun is, Mr Winkler?"

He turned to the bed and continued "... and the latest news is, that I have just decided to shoot the father instead of his pretty wife."

Mr Jacobvic was now lying on the bed, with his hands and feet tied behind his back, and his mouth covered.

Slowly, Mr Meier took his gun out of his pocket and pointed it at Mr Jacobvic's back. "Time to die big man," he said. "I would say it was nice getting to know you, but that would be a lie."

"Don't do it!" Officer Winkler shouted on the phone. "Mr Meier, please! Together we can still find a solution!"

Mr Meier smiled. "Mr Winkler, today you've made me laugh. And believe me, that's not easy to do. You did your best. Now go home, read a good book and relax!"

"You want me to relax and read a book? How can I do that if you have just shot a woman?"

"Well then, go home and put your feet in cold water!"

The weapon was still pointing at Mr Jacobvic, as he carefully ended the call.

Petra cried loudly.

Mr Meier took one step closer and pressed the gun against Mr Jacobvic's head.

"Good night," said Mr Meier quietly. He looked away, so that he would get as little blood on his body as possible.

He quickly put the gun back into his pocket.

"Good decision," said the commissioner. She was standing in the doorway and Mr Meier had only just noticed her.

The commissioner closed the door and without another word, she began approaching Mr Meier, with her gun pointed at him.

She came closer and closer.

"Hmmm hmmm hmmm!" warned Mr Jacobvic.

But despite the warning, she continued approaching until her weapon pressed against Mr Meier's chest. "You thought you were smarter than us, eh?" she asked him.

She held the back of his head and started to kiss him, as he put his arms tightly around her body.

The two kissed each other, as if their mouths were in a fight.

Still kissing, they fell against the wall and then against the door. They kissed next to the tied-up Petra Jacobvic, who was still lying helpless on the ground. They continued to kiss and with so much passion that they both eventually fell on to the bed. Only then did they stop.

Breathless, the commissioner lay comfortably on the bed, with her back pressed against the tied-up Mr Jacobvic. "Happy birthday to you!" she sang with a sweet voice.

"Thank you, Tanja," he replied.

She sat down, put the gun back into her pocket and continued: "Normally, when someone has a birthday, they eat cake and drink a lot of beer, but you're something else! A gun and a tied-up couple?... Man!"

Mr Meier sat next to her on the bed. "Well... what can I say? I wanted to see you again and knew you were going to come somehow." He gently kissed her on her neck.

"Umm... that's right, but next time you can just send me a private email with a false name!"

"Oh Tanja, I don't care about computer technology and you know I like a good game!"

"Yes... I know that well. So, let's get to the point because we only have ten minutes here..."

Mr Meier smiled and rubbed his hands, "Aaaah, for my birthday present we're going to throw the couple in the wardrobe, so that you and I can enjoy five or six minutes on this bed!"

"NO! I mean, we all have to get out of here now!"

"Oh..." said Mr Meier, rather disappointed. "That's a pity and I thought..."

SMASH!

Tanja, the commissioner, suddenly fell forward from the bed onto the floor. Unfortunately, she and Mr Meier hadn't notice that Petra Jacobvic was free again.

She had hit the commissioner on the head with the broken alarm clock.

7. SIX MINUTES

Before Mr Meier could move, Petra took the gun out of Tanja's pocket and pointed it at her.

"Stay where you are, and I won't shoot your girlfriend!" she warned him.

"Okay, okay... stay calm, stay calm!" said Mr Meier quietly.

"Hands up!" she shouted.

"*Hands up*? Oh man, you've been watching too many thrillers on your damn TV!"

"Shut your mouth and don't move!"

"*Don't move or hands up*? What exactly do you want?" he asked.

But Petra didn't let herself get confused by his questions. She ignored him and with her free hand, she took a piece of glass from the alarm clock and cut through the ropes of her tied-up husband. He was quickly freed from all the ropes.

Mr Jacobvic immediately took the gun from Mr Meier's pocket.

"Get on the bed!" shouted Petra. Tanja slowly got up and sat down next to Mr Meier again. She wiped away a little blood that was on her head.

Tanja turned to her friend. "I have to tell you something..."

"Yes? What is it?"

"... it's never boring with you," she said, laughing quietly. "Never!"

Mr Meier also began to quietly laugh. "That's true," he said, looking up at the ceiling. Suddenly he looked back at her, with a serious face again. "Tell me... how is Jürgen?"

"Shut up!" Mr Jacobvic shouted and punched Mr Meier in the face. "You wanted to hurt my wife? I'll show you!" Angrily, he searched for more rope. Then he got the tape from the floor and also a knife from the kitchen.

"Take this for a minute," he said, and gave his wife the gun.

Now with both hands free, he lifted Tanja up in the air, turned her around and placed her with her face and stomach back down on the bed. "That's how you treat a goose at Christmas!" he said.

"What are you doing?" she asked, rather shocked. "You want to tie me up? Are you serious? You can't do that!"

"Oh yes I can", said Mr Jacobvic, pushing a longer piece of rope under her body.

"No!" Tanja shouted. "Stop! Don't you know who I am? I... I am the commissioner of the Danburg Police!"

"Yeah, and I'm Harry Potter," Mr Jacobvic replied quietly as he tightly tied her hands behind her back, just as Mr Meier had done to him and his wife.

"It's the truth! I'm really the commissioner!" she protested. "Look in my bag! I'm really from the police!"

"Oh yeah?" said Mr Jacobvic. "A policewoman with a short skirt and low-cut top? You're lying!"

"I'm not lying! We don't always wear uniforms in situations like this!" she explained. "Look in my bag. If you can't find any evidence, you can shoot me right away! Okay?"

The couple looked at each other.

With the gun still in her hand, Petra searched in Tanja's handbag.

"Well?" asked Mr Jacobvic.

Petra kept looking but said nothing.

"Darling... Is it true?" asked Mr Jacobvic, "Is this witch really a policewoman?"

"It looks like it," Petra replied quietly. "This ID card is genuine. But she's not just a policewoman, she's the commissioner."

"Yes, and you're not criminals…" said Tanja, "but in six minutes everything will be over for all of us…"

"What do you mean?" asked Petra.

"In six minutes, lots of heavily armed police officers will storm in here. Either they'll shoot you right away, or at least three of us will end up in jail!"

"But why?" asked Petra. "We were kidnapped!"

"I don't care!" said Tanja. "When the police get here and see me, their *wonderful boss,* on this bed, tied with my hands and feet behind my back... how can you explain that?"

"But..."

"And your fingerprints are all over my gun... how are you going to explain that?"

"But..."

Tanja continued: "... maybe I'll be fired from my job because I came here alone... but Mr Jacobvic will have to take care of the children... without their mother."

"And he's unemployed," said Mr Meier, slowly clapping his hands.

"But we're innocent!" the parents protested together.

"Listen to me...." said Tanja aloud, "either we can all get out of here quickly, as if nothing had happened, or you can wait here for the armed police to arrive and then I'll have to tell them the truth, that you hit me and then tied me up. If you take the second choice, then the mother won't see her children for three or four years."

Tanja quickly looked at the clock on the wall. "Now we only have five minutes left. Make your decision quickly!"

For a moment, the couple thought about what to do.

"She's right..." Petra finally said to her husband. "We all should get out of here, right now!"

"Wait a moment!" said Mr Jacobvic suddenly. Everybody looked at him.

"But you only have a few minutes to let me go! What's the matter now?" asked Tanja angrily.

"I want you to get me a job... something in an office maybe... but not in Danburg! Leipzig or Dresden would be okay. And we also want this pig (he pointed his finger at Mr Meier) to move far away from us. He has to go somewhere else!"

Mr Meier laughed loudly. "Do it for him," he told Tanja. "Better than if we both go to prison!"

"Yeah, okay, I promise," said Tanja annoyed. "You have my word. Now hurry up and let me go. This rope is really hurting me!"

Mr Meier got up and walked quickly to the door. Suddenly he turned around again.

"Tanja, I really want to know... how is Jürgen doing?"

"Jürgen is fine... now go!"

Mr Meier shook his head and left the room.

Mr Jacobvic cut through Tanja's ropes and she was free again. She stood up immediately.

"Go and get your children," she told Mr Jacobvic. "I'll call the police now and tell them that I've found the woman alone and unharmed."

"Yeah, the cafe is closing soon," he said. He kissed his wife and quickly left the room, closing the door as he went.

Tanja turned to Petra. "Mrs Jacobvic, do you want to explain to the police, why you have my gun?"

"Oh dear!" said Petra and quickly gave her back her weapon.

"And?" asked Tanja.

"And what? Oh... Mr Meier's weapon! Here please take it!" Petra gave back the other weapon to Tanja. She immediately put them both in her handbag.

"And now you're going to use your phone?" asked Petra.

"Yes..." replied Tanja, "... exactly."

"*What an evening*!" thought Petra with relief. The nightmare was finally over. She couldn't wait to see her children again.

As soon as she could get her phone switched back on, she would call them!

Tanja sat down on the bed again and wiped a bit of dirt from off her skirt.

"Well?" asked Petra. "What are you waiting for?"

8. THE FIRST NIGHT

Tanja paused, while looking for more dirt on her skirt. "Do you like my clothes?" she finally asked Petra.

"Er... yes... it's pretty," Petra replied politely.

"Pretty? Is that all? This short skirt alone cost me 95 euros!"

"Quality costs," answered Petra, still being polite.

"Yes... *quality costs*. This tiny pink and black top cost 75 euros but it's my favourite... and you don't think that my high-heeled shoes are too high for a woman of my appearance?"

"Yes... err, I *mean no*... it looks great... Oh, are you calling the police now? I would like to go and..."

"Oh dear!" interrupted Tanja, "I almost forgot... at any moment lots of big men will come in, and I'm sitting on this elegant bed, wearing only a short red skirt and a low-cut top!" She looked up at Petra. "Don't you find that a bit exciting, Mrs Jacobvic?"

"Excuse me?" answered Petra, not sure what to say.

"Oh yeah... you're Eastern European... that's obvious."

"You're scaring me."

"May I call you *Petra?*" asked Tanja. She slowly leaned back on the bed, while her eyes stayed fixed on the other woman.

"Er... my name is Mrs Jacobvic."

"Petra..." began Tanja regardless, "I have to tell you something about myself..."

"What... what do you want to tell me?"

Tanja stood up and slowly took a few steps towards Petra.

"Sometimes I'm a crazy woman."

"Re... really?" asked Petra. She took a step backwards.

"Yes...really. The SEK leader also called me that a short time ago..."

Tanja slowly approached Petra, but Petra took a few more steps backwards.

"I need help Petra..." said Tanja. "I need help because I've always found danger to be exciting. The more danger that I'm in, the more exciting I find it."

Petra took another step backwards, but then felt the wall against her back.

Tanja slowly continued to step nearer. "Petra...", she began, "you're an intelligent woman. You know what would happen if you said something about me or my friend Mr Meier?"

"Yes, I am an intelligent woman and I know what would happen if I... If I said something about you or your friend Mr Meier," Petra repeated with fear.

"Hey, hey. . . Petra Baby!" said Tanja, suddenly with a sweet and caring voice. "Honey... don't be afraid of me. Everything is going to be fine. Please! I want... I want this moment to be special."

"What are you saying? What moment?"

"Petra, I came here, because I wanted to see Mr Meier again, but to be honest, that wasn't my only reason. Three salespeople and Mr Meier talked about your great beauty. I didn't believe them. But now that I can see you with my own eyes, I know that they were all telling the truth."

"Er, thank you, but my children are waiting for me now and I've..."

"Petra... have you ever kissed a woman in your life?" asked Tanja.

"*Kissed a woman?* No, of course not. Why are you asking me that? Oh... Oh no! Please don't think about that!"

But Tanja stepped even closer. The distance between them was now less than an arm's length. "Petra, about 25 years ago, I promised myself that if I were ever to kiss a woman in my life, she would have to be the most beautiful woman that I've ever seen."

"Why are you telling me that?"

"Because today is that day and you are that woman."

"Please no, please no!" said Petra, shaking her head.

Tanja took her last step forward, so that their noses could touch each other.

"Petra..." said Tanja quietly, "I've risked a lot in my life to become the commissioner and now I am risking it all just to kiss you. Close your beautiful eyes and just think *of the first night*... the first night that you finally spent alone with your husband..."

"*The first night?*" asked Petra.

"Yes... and now, instead of your husband, kiss me with the same passion. With the passion that says: *At last I have you alone and only for me!*"

Petra slowly closed her eyes. Before all the arguing, before the marriage, and even before they were a couple, she would have done anything to spend five minutes with Fillip Jacobvic.

She was sixteen, very much in love but also very unhappy. Mum and Dad had banned Filip from meeting her several times. Dad had warned Filip's father: "If your son comes near my daughter again, someone will definitely end up in the hospital!"

Petra would cry into her pillow almost every day, but this day was going to end very differently.

It was eleven o'clock at night and her parents were sleeping.

Earlier in the day, she had wiped the window frame of her second-floor bedroom with oil, so it wouldn't make any noise. She slowly opened the window and began to carefully go through it, so that she could climb down the nearby tree.

But she hadn't planned the next step so well. The tree wasn't us near as she thought. She stretched out a hand, further and further, but she couldn't reach it... and then she slipped.

"Help! Help!" she cried, as she hung helplessly from her window frame. Her fingers were a bit oily and she couldn't hold on much longer. She was about to fall six meters to the ground.

The light in her bedroom was suddenly turned on and two big hands quickly pulled her back into the room.

"Are you crazy?" her angry dad shouted. He noticed that his hands were oily and knew immediately what his daughter had

done. Angrily, he turned around and punched the wall hard. Although Petra was supposed to be grateful, she fell to her knees and cried hysterically.

Throughout the next day, she cried a lot more than before. She didn't eat and her parents wouldn't talk to her.

The following morning Petra was still in her bedroom, looking sadly through the window, when the parents came in and ordered her to pack some of her clothes.

"Hurry up!" was all that the mum would say.

"What are we going to do?" she asked anxiously.

"Just get in the car," said the dad, without looking at her.

The three of them got into the car and drove off.

"Where are we going?" asked Petra. Her mum looked quickly at her husband. He shook his head for a moment, and they continued the journey without talking. The daughter was confused.

They drove through the city, under the main bridge, around the town hall and then she saw it... the hospital.

A tear rolled down her face.

"Dad... I'm really sorry! Forgive me!" she cried. "I'm not a crazy person!"

But the car drove past the hospital, still without any words from the parents.

"But...?" she said, turning around to see the hospital getting further and further behind them.

A few minutes later, the car drove past a church that she felt she had seen before. She was staring at it, as the car began to slow down.

Her dad parked the car and turned to his daughter, looking calm but serious: "Petra, never forget how much we love you, okay? Now please get out."

"But..."

"GET OUT! GET OUT!" he screamed and angrily wiped away a tear.

Petra quickly got out of the car. Her mother followed and together they walked a few meters away from the car.

"Mother, I don't understand what's going on. Why...?"

But her mother didn't let her finish talking. She hugged her daughter tightly and then looked at her very seriously. "Honey, listen to me... it's almost two o'clock. The pharmacy is around the corner and open until eight o'clock. Here's money for that as well as for something to eat. You can also buy a travel card for tomorrow from it. Look... over there; Filip is in his car waiting for you... go now!"

She kissed her speechless daughter on the head and walked back to her husband's car.

The car drove very quickly away.

Petra's parents had finally realised that they couldn't protect their daughter every minute of the day and that it would be safer for her to be able to meet her boyfriend Filip whenever, rather than for her to secretly risk her life.

And so almost 8 hours later 'The First Night' finally took place. They had had something to eat and also had drank some alcohol. The two were now alone in Filip's small room. "No

Petra's back was pushed against the wall. Their noses gently met.

Still standing, they kissed. They kissed long and very, very slowly. A few tears of happiness rolled down Petra's face and dripped onto her partner's foot, as they continue to slowly kiss.

At last, they both stopped. Neither person moved and for a few seconds there was just silence. Only their two beating hearts could be heard...

"Oh yes!" said Tanja finally and almost out of breath. "That was amazing!"

9. THE END?

Petra opened her eyes and was suddenly back in reality. She was shocked and started to shiver as she realised what she had just done.

"Please!" she begged, as more tears fell on Tanja's feet. "I've done what you wanted, please call the police now!"

"That won't be necessary," said Tanja.

"Why not?" asked Petra, frustrated.

Suddenly, Tanja's knee hit Petra's stomach, fast and very hard.

"AAAAARGHHH!" screamed Petra in great pain. She fell heavily to the ground. BOOM! Was the sound her body made as she landed.

"Nobody hits me and gets away with it," said the commissioner, no longer with a sweet voice. "Do you really think I forgot about the alarm clock?" She stepped hard on Petra's hand.

The commissioner quickly collected the few pieces of the broken alarm clock and put them in her bag. She got on her knees and wiped her light purple coloured lipstick from Petra's mouth with a tissue.

Then the commissioner got up again and looked at the door.

Four SEK policemen with weapons ran into the room. Red laser beams immediately pointed at the two women.

"Sir, the two women are here!" they shouted. "They're here! Thanks to the scream, we finally found them!"

"My stomach, my stomach...!" Petra whispered over and over, whilst rolling back and forth on the floor.

"Where's the man?" one of the SEK policemen asked the commissioner.

"I have no idea..." she replied, "... he hit me, but despite my head injury I hit him back and after that, he ran away. Unfortunately, the man had his face covered the whole time."

"You hit him? commissioner, what a heroine you are! But are you really ok?"

"Never better, thank you." She replied with a little smile. "Everything went just as I would have dreamed."

And that's how this story ended.

Or did it?

Of course, Petra Jacobvic was taken to the hospital and two months later she felt better. Her stomach only hurts a little when she laughs too much.

Above all, she is glad that she can now eat proper food and no longer has to just drink protein drinks!

The parents don't argue as much as they used to, but whenever they do, it never lasts long. They agreed that the whole family should hug each other every night before going to bed, whether they are happy or not... how sweet!

They also threw all of Thomas and Markus' computer games away.

The boys don't miss the games as much as they had expected to. Thomas is now eleven years old and often plays football or basketball with his friends in the park. Markus, who is three years older, doesn't find his female classmates as stupid or boring as they used to be.

He has no idea why.

Back to Petra: A year has passed, and with her eight years of experience as a model, she started her own modelling agency. She is hopeful that in 16 years' time, her daughter will work with her (she is now pregnant and expecting a daughter).

And what happened to Officer Winkler? Sometimes he still thinks about Mr Meier. The officer still can't understand something that the caller had said to him... *"Put your feet in cold water..."* where had he heard this crazy phrase before?

"Oh, forget it!" Sandra said to him annoyed. "The most important thing I've learned in five years with the police, is that you shouldn't ask too many stupid questions..."

She continued: "... and now come to bed! Tomorrow we have to get up early!"

59

THE END

Before you go!

I'd really appreciate if you left a review on Amazon.

Find more of my books in English, German, Spanish and even French at JASI.ONLINE

And don't forget to subscribe, so that I can keep you up to date.

Michael Wolliston

A special thanks to -

Sabrina Schmidt

& Jordan Whittaker

This book is dedicated to my past mum and dad.

Without them, writing this book wouldn't have been possible.